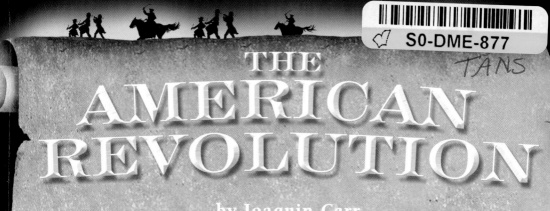

THE AMERICAN REVOLUTION

by Joaquin Carr

Table of Contents

INTRODUCTION

From the early 1600s to the middle 1700s, people from Europe settled along the east coast of the United States. Most were from Britain.

Over time, the settled areas became thirteen different **colonies** ruled by Britain and British laws. Most colonists were proud to be a part of Britain. But the British king, George III, began to control the colonies more and more.

By the 1760s, many colonists couldn't stand the king's tight control. He sent troops to watch everything. He put heavy taxes on many of the goods bought from other countries.

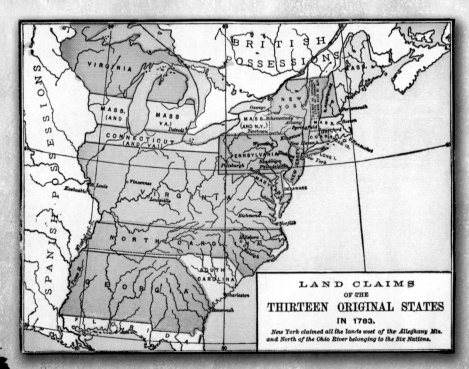

LAND CLAIMS
OF THE
THIRTEEN ORIGINAL STATES
IN 1783.

New York claimed all the lands west of the Alleghany Mts. and North of the Ohio River belonging to the Six Nations.

▲ the original thirteen colonies in 1763

Trouble grew. In Massachusetts, colonists fought with British soldiers. The fighting spread to other colonies and slowly built to a war.

Why did so many colonists **rebel** against the king? How did the colonists win their **independence**? How did the thirteen colonies become one new nation—the United States of America?

In this book, you'll learn what caused the American Revolution. You'll read about key people and battles You'll see how untrained soldiers and regular people with a dream of freedom defeated the mighty British army.

◀ Colonists met to discuss unfair British taxes.

BEFORE THE WAR
(1765–1773)

THE STAMP ACT

In March 1765, the British government passed a law called the Stamp Act. It forced colonists to pay taxes on any printed item they bought from Britain. This meant books, calendars, playing cards, and many more everyday items would be taxed. The colonists were angry.

The British said the taxes would pay for British troops who protected the colonists. But many colonists objected. They had no representatives (reh-pree-ZEHN-tuh-tivz) in the British government. They felt that Britain had no right to force more taxes on them without their vote.

Primary Source

Declaration of Rights
In October 1765, representatives from nine colonies met. They sent King George III a list of thirteen rights they felt were theirs.
Number Five said:
"That the only representatives of the people of these colonies are persons chosen by themselves; and that no taxes ever have been or can be constitutionally imposed on them but by their respective legislatures."

Many colonists disagreed with the Stamp Act. They said that they would not buy British goods. Some colonists simply refused to pay the taxes. Others burned stamps or destroyed the building where taxes were collected. These actions did not got unnoticed. By 1766, the king put an end to the Stamp Act.

▲ Angry colonists burned stamps to show their unhappiness with the Stamp Act.

THE BOSTON MASSACRE

Even after the Stamp Act ended, many colonists still objected to the king's strict rules. They wouldn't buy British goods. The king sent 4,000 British soldiers to keep order in Boston. The soldiers also kept ships from sailing in and out of Boston Harbor. The colonists could no longer trade goods with other nations.

On the night of March 5, 1770, a mob of colonists threw snowballs at British soldiers. A shoving match followed. Then it turned deadly. A few British soldiers fired their guns into the crowd. By the time the last shot was fired, three colonists lay dead. Later, two more colonists died from their wounds.

This event became known as the Boston Massacre. The colonists who did not want to obey the king's rule became known as **rebels** (REH-buhlz).

Crispus Attucks

Crispus Attucks was the first of the five colonists killed in the Boston Massacre. He had escaped slavery twenty years before. He spent many of his free years as a sailor on whaling ships. In Boston, he worked as a rope maker. In 1888, a Crispus Attucks monument was set in Boston Common.

Crispus Attucks

6

Primary Source

After the Boston Massacre, a silversmith named Paul Revere made a poster about it. He printed many copies and hung them all around Boston. His poster showed British troops shooting colonists on command. That is not how it really happened. The poster purposely stretched the truth to stir up the colonists' anger.

Historical Perspective

Even today posters, banners, and and other types of advertising stretch the truth to get people to take action.

THE BOSTON TEA PARTY

In 1773, the British government passed a law called the Tea Act. The new law made tea cheaper to buy. So why did the law upset so many colonists?

Only one company would be allowed to send tea to the colonies. The colonists didn't think one company should control the sale of their favorite drink.

On the night of December 16, 1773, thousands of colonists went to a Boston church. They didn't go to hear a preacher. They went to hear a rebel named Samuel Adams. He thought that the British government had gone too far. He asked his listeners to take action.

And take action they did! To **protest** (proh-TEHST), many of Adams' listeners dressed up as Mohawks. Quietly, they boarded three ships that carried crates of British tea. They dumped the crates into Boston Harbor. This **protest** (PROH-tehst) became known as the Boston Tea Party. King George III was furious.

1. Solve This

During the Boston Tea Party, men threw 342 crates of tea overboard. Each crate carried about 263 pounds of tea. About how many pounds of tea were dumped into the harbor?

▲ To protest the Tea Act, angry colonists dumped British tea into Boston Harbor.

THE REVOLUTION HEATS UP (1774–1776)

After the Boston Tea Party, the king shut down Boston Harbor. He took away most of the local government's control. And the colonists took action.

In September 1774, fifty-six representatives from twelve colonies met at the First **Continental Congress** (KON-teh-NEHN-tuhl KON-grihs) in Philadelphia.

Patriots wanted to break away from British rule.

Loyalists, who supported the king, wanted the colonies to get along with Britain.

Finally, Congress wrote a letter to King George III and the British people. It listed the colonists' problems with the British government. It asked British citizens to help the colonists. Together they might find ways to make peace with the king.

▼ The First Continental Congress met in September 1774.

LEXINGTON AND CONCORD

On the night of April 18, 1775, any last chance of peace with Britain ended. The British had learned that colonists were collecting guns and supplies in Lexington and Concord, towns near Boston. The British ordered 700 soldiers to find the men and take them prisoner.

Before the British could get to Lexington, Patriots Paul Revere and William Dawes raced out on horseback in the middle of the night. They cried out, "The British are coming!" They wanted to wake up Patriot troops. These troops were called Minutemen because they could be ready to fight very quickly.

The next day, at dawn, seventy Minutemen and 600 British soldiers fought each other in Lexington. No one is certain who fired first. Patriot leaders John Hancock and Sam Adams escaped.

Although the Minutemen lost the short battle, other colonists moved the supplies in Concord to safety. Along the way, they, too, got into a fight with the British.

The fighting at Lexington and Concord started a long war between Britain and the colonies. It came to be known as the American Revolution.

The Second Continental Congress met in May 1775. The king had not answered their letter. The fighting at Lexington and Concord showed that both the Patriots and the British were serious.

With a war brewing, the Congress created the Continental Army. They asked war-hero George Washington to lead.

The Congress also asked each colony for money to pay for the war. Secretly, some Patriots went to get help for their cause from friendly European nations.

The Second Continental Congress sent another letter to King George III, asking for a peaceful end to the fighting.

In part the letter said, "We think ourselves required . . . to use all the means in our power. . . for stopping the further effusion [spilling] of blood."

But it reached the king too late.

The Battle of Bunker Hill, near Boston, took place in June 1775. More than 1,000 of the king's soldiers were killed or hurt. He sent more troops to the colonies and called on American Indian tribes for support. The king knew they were angry at the colonists for settling on Indian land.

COMMON SENSE;

ADDRESSED TO THE

INHABITANTS

OF

AMERICA,

On the following interesting

SUBJECTS.

I. Of the Origin and Design of Government in general, with concise Remarks on the English Constitution.

II. Of Monarchy and Hereditary Succession.

III. Thoughts on the present State of American Affairs.

IV. Of the present Ability of America, with some miscellaneous Reflections.

Man knows no Master save creating HEAVEN,
Or those whom choice and common good ordain.
THOMSON.

PHILADELPHIA;
Printed, and Sold, by R. BELL, in Third-Street.
MDCCLXXVI.

By the spring of 1776, many colonists had read a **pamphlet** (PAM-flit) by Thomas Paine called "Common Sense." This short paper persuaded many colonists that they should break away from British rule.

Many colonists now wanted to be independent. The Congress wrote a formal statement: "Resolved: That these united colonies ought to be free and independent states." This means that people have the right to choose how they are governed.

Primary Source

Common Sense
"We have it in our power to begin the world anew. It is the opportunity to bring forward a system of government in which the rights of all men should be preserved, that gives value to independence. America shall make a stand, not for herself alone, but for the world."

Thomas Paine didn't get a penny for writing his best-selling essay. He gave all of his profits to help the colonies gain their independence.

THE DECLARATION OF INDEPENDENCE

Then the Congress gave Patriot Thomas Jefferson the writing job of his life. They asked him to write a Declaration of Independence (deh-kluh-RAY-shun ov ihn-duh-PEHN-duhns). He was assisted by fellow Patriots Benjamin Franklin and John Adams. Jefferson presented this historic document to the Second Continental Congress. It made three big points:

1. All people are born with certain rights that cannot be taken away.

2. King George III did not respect the colonists' rights.

3. So, the colonies had a right to break away from the British government.

The Second Continental Congress approved. The Declaration of Independence was passed on July 4, 1776. When the Declaration of Independence was approved, Congress became a formal governing body. It set the direction of a brand new nation.

"All men are created equal . . . with the right to Life, Liberty, and the Pursuit of Happiness."

the Declaration of Independence ▶

▲ General Washington led his troops to victory after crossing the Delaware River.

In spring 1776, while the Second Continental Congress was meeting, George Washington faced a huge challenge. More than 30,000 British troops were about to invade New York. Washington's Continental Army had only 14,500 untrained men.

By fall 1776, the Continental Army had lost many battles. But the Declaration of Independence had been signed, and General Washington wasn't ready to give up. His strategy was to keep his men moving. Though many were hungry and sick, they marched from New York City all the way to Pennsylvania.

Washington knew that a group of German soldiers was helping the British. Those soldiers had camped out in Trenton, New Jersey, just across the river from Washington's army.

Late Christmas night, in 1776, General Washington and his troops quietly rowed across the Delaware River. At dawn, the Patriots made a sneak attack and won. They took more than 900 prisoners.

THE WAR WAGES ON
(1777–1779)

General Washington's victory at Trenton boosted the Patriots' hopes. Just one week later, Washington scored another victory. On January 2, 1777, he lit campfires to make it look like his men were resting. But his troops were really already marching to Princeton, New Jersey. There, they surprised and defeated a group of soldiers led by British General Charles Cornwallis (korn-WAH-lihs).

The Continental Army didn't have much else to cheer about in the coming months. In July 1777, the British defeated Patriot forces at Fort Ticonderoga (TIGH-kon-duh-ROH-gah) in New York. Not long after that, Washington's troops were beaten again in two major battles. By the fall, the British had taken control of Philadelphia, the capital of the thirteen colonies.

◀ This painting shows the British taking over Philadelphia. Americans nicknamed the British "redcoats" for the color of the soldiers' uniforms.

▲ By giving his sword to the Americans, General Burgoyne agreed to give up fighting.

British General John Burgoyne (buhr-GOIN) wanted to cut off trade and communication between the colonies in the north and the other colonies. If he could divide the Patriot forces, they'd be defeated.

But the Patriots didn't give up. In Vermont, colonists melted down their metal spoons and dinner plates. They used the metal to make homemade bullets.

The Patriots fought a fierce battle at Saratoga, New York.

Then, on October 17, 1777, Burgoyne gave up.

The Battle of Saratoga was the greatest win yet for the Patriots. It was a turning point in the Revolution, too. The victory stopped the British plan to cut off the North from the rest of the colonies. For the first time, other countries in Europe began to believe that the Americans might have a chance to win. The Patriots knew they would need outside help to succeed.

Point

Read More About It

You can read more about the battles of Fort Ticonderoga and Saratoga at your school media center. An adult can help you search the Internet for information and primary sources.

They Made a Difference

Heroic colonists worked hard for the cause of liberty. Many, such as Sybil Ludington, were women.

One night in 1777, a Patriot messenger arrived at the house where sixteen-year-old Sybil lived. He told Sybil's father that the British were going to attack an important **militia** (muh-LIHSH-uh) supply center fifteen miles away. The militia was an army of regular people called for battle when needed.

While Sybil's father, a well-known militia officer, got ready, Sybil volunteered to warn his men. In the dark of night, she rode her horse for forty miles on roads she did not know.

The militia arrived at the supply center just in time to push the British back. Later, a grateful General Washington visited Sybil, thanking her personally for her bravery.

▲ Just like Paul Revere's, Sybil Ludington's "midnight ride" helped the Patriot troops.

THE WINTER AT VALLEY FORGE

While the Patriots cheered at Saratoga, General Washington's army sunk to its lowest point as winter approached. Washington's troops were running out of clothing and food.

Washington set up camp for the winter about twenty miles (32 kilometers) from Philadelphia, at a place called Valley Forge. Many of his troops marched there without shoes. The cuts in their feet left trails of blood on the frozen ground.

In the winter of 1777–78, the ▶ most brutal foe Washington's army battled was not the British, but the weather.

The soldiers were tired when they reached Valley Forge. But they did not dare to rest. They needed to build log huts to keep warm in the cold months ahead. Since their horses were too weak to haul wood, the troops dragged the logs themselves.

Washington was troubled by the hardships his troops faced at Valley Forge. He did not move into the large house provided for him right away. Instead he slept in a tent until his men had finished building their huts.

Primary Source

All winter, Washington wrote letters to the Second Continental Congress. He begged them to send food and clothing. Here is part of one letter: "I am now convinced, beyond a doubt, that unless some great change takes place, this Army must . . . be reduced to one or other of these three things. Starve, dissolve (dih-sawlv), or disperse (dih-spers); rest assured, Sir, I have reason to support what I say."

▼ Washington's troops had to build more than 1,200 huts at Valley Forge. Twelve soldiers slept in each hut in bunks with three levels.

Sadly, even the new shelters were not enough. During the awful winter that followed, nearly one out of every four men died from illness or hunger.

The troops who did survive Valley Forge became a stronger fighting force. Washington had brought in German captain Baron von Steuben (VAHN STOO-bin)

to give them better training. The captain taught the Patriots how to load their rifles correctly. He also changed the way the army marched. The Patriots had been marching in long straight lines, like the British. Now they learned to move in quicker, shorter lines.

▲ Baron von Steuben trained the Continental Army to be better fighters.

▲ King Louis XVI admired and respected Benjamin Franklin.

By spring 1778, the men's spirits improved, and so did the weather. The Continental Army was eager to test out its new training.

At the same time, the Patriots were about to get a new **ally** (AH-ligh), or partner, in the war.

Benjamin Franklin was in France trying to get King Louis XVI to help the Patriot war effort. The colonists' victory at Saratoga caught the attention of the French king. In May 1778, he agreed to send French troops and money to help the colonies win their independence.

THE WAR MOVES SOUTH

When the British army left Philadelphia, Washington's army pursued them. The two sides battled in Monmouth, New Jersey. There was no clear winner, but Washington's troops did very well. Their training at Valley Forge had sharpened their skills.

At the same time, the British changed their war plan. They began to move south. They wanted to be sure that Britain kept the rich farmland in the South. They also wanted to take the seacoast. Then they could control all trade.

The British captured Savannah, Georgia, in December 1778. The Patriots were worried. Would the new British strategy mean the end of the dream of independence?

▼ More than 10,000 slaves were awarded their freedom for fighting in the American Revolution.

It's a Fact

By 1779, one out of seven soldiers in Washington's army was African American. Many were slaves who were promised freedom after the war ended.

THE WAR WINDS DOWN
(1780–1783)

The British continued their march through the South in spring 1780. They captured Charleston, South Carolina.

That same year, the Patriots received another blow. They discovered that Benedict Arnold, one of their own generals, gave their secrets to the British. Arnold helped the British plan to capture West Point, New York. Luckily, the Patriots uncovered the plan.

It's a Fact

Before Benedict Arnold switched sides, he was a Patriot hero. He won several battles for the Continental Army.

After the Americans ▶ learned about his plot, Benedict Arnold escaped and fought with the British.

Then the British plan began to fall apart. Patriot General Nathanael Greene fought frequently against British troops in the South. Far more British troops than Patriots were killed or hurt.

In March 1781, the British were badly defeated at a battle in North Carolina. British General Cornwallis was forced to make a move he would soon regret.

2. Solve This

Soldiers in the Continental Army only earned $6.67 each month. Exactly how much would a soldier make in one year's time?

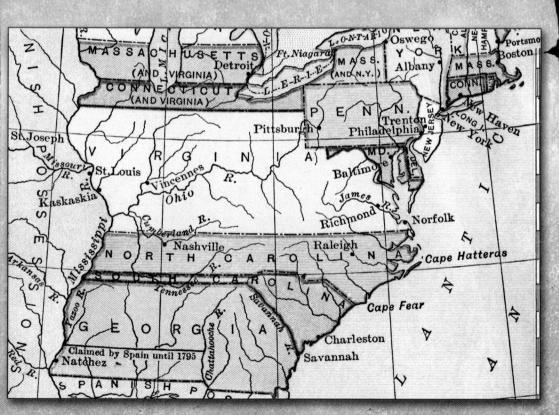

▲ Key battles toward the end of the war took place in the southern colonies.

In May 1781, Cornwallis headed to Virginia. He ordered his army to set up camp in Yorktown on the Chesapeake (CHEHS-uh-peek) Bay, where it would be easy to unload supplies. Cornwallis thought that more British troops and fresh supplies would soon arrive to help him.

Meanwhile, French troops had finally arrived to help the Patriots.

▲ Admiral Francois de Grasse commanded the French fleet heading to Virginia.

▲ At Yorktown, Cornwallis counted on getting more help from Britain.

French ships commanded by Admiral Francois de Grasse were headed toward the Chesapeake Bay. Washington and French general Compte de Rochambeau (KONT deh raw-shum-BOH) decided to join forces and trap Cornwallis and his men at Yorktown.

Washington knew there were already 4,000 Patriot troops stationed near Yorktown. Together, the French and Patriot troops and the French fleet would be powerful. In fact, they would outnumber Cornwallis's troops three to one!

French and Patriot troops marched south from New York. The French fleet arrived in Virginia on August 31, 1781. When the British realized that Cornwallis was in trouble, they sent ships to Yorktown to rescue him. But the French fleet was stronger. It turned away the British ships with cannon fire.

▲ The British and Patriot armies fought a long battle in Yorktown, Virginia, in 1781.

▲ When the British surrendered their weapons at Yorktown, Cornwallis did not attend. He claimed to be sick.

VICTORY AT YORKTOWN

Fierce fighting continued for weeks. In October, Washington gave the command to fire cannons and guns at will on the British troops in Yorktown. The Patriots and French fired almost around the clock.

The British did not have a chance to regroup. After a week of constant attacks, Cornwallis's army fell apart. Most of his men were sick or wounded. Plus, they were surrounded. The Patriot and French troops cut off escape by land. The French fleet sealed off escape by sea.

Cornwallis knew his army would be defeated. So he gave up. The British were marched out of Yorktown as prisoners on October 20, 1781.

Point

Reread

Reread pages 28-29. Name at least one good decision General Washington made that helped the Patriots win the war.

The Patriots had captured the largest British army in the colonies. A new British government decided that a war in the colonies was no longer worth fighting.

In June 1781, a committee from the Second Continental Congress began peace talks with the British. Benjamin Franklin played a key role in making peace.

The peace talks took more than two years. On September 3, 1783, the British and Americans signed the Treaty of Paris in France. This treaty ended the Revolutionary War. Britain recognized the independent United States of America.

▲ In this relief sculpture, Benjamin Franklin (standing) is about to sign the Treaty of Paris.

CONCLUSION

The American Revolution was a long and difficult war. When it was over, exhausted and ragged American soldiers returned to their families to enjoy their new-found and hard-fought freedom.

The Patriots never gave up their dream of independence. Their courage, along with soldiers and supplies from other countries, made the victory possible. Use the time line to review key moments in the Revolution. How did each step move the colonists closer to winning the right to govern themselves?

Time Line of the American Revolution

1765

March 1765:
The Stamp Act

March 1770:
The Boston Massacre

December 1773:
The Boston Tea Party

September 1774:
First Continental Congress meets.

April 1775:
With the battles of Lexington and Concord, the American Revolution begins.

January 1776:
Thomas Paine writes "Common Sense."

July 4, 1776:
The Declaration of Independence is adopted.

October 1776:
The Patriots win the Battle of Saratoga.

Winter 1777–78:
Patriot forces winter at Valley Forge.

Spring 1778:
France supports the Patriot cause.

October 1781:
Patriot and French forces win at Yorktown.

September 1783:
A peace treaty is signed, ending the war.

1783

GLOSSARY

ally — (AH-ligh) a partner or supporter (page 22)

colony — (KAHL-uh-nee) a land claimed and ruled by a country far away (page 2)

Continental Congress — (KON-teh-NEHN-tuhl KON-grihs) a formal meeting of representatives from the colonies (page 10)

independence — (ihn-duh-PEHN-duhns) ruling or governing oneself (page 3)

Loyalist — (LOY-uh-lihst) a colonist who continued to support the king of England (page 10)

militia — (muh-LIHSH-uh) an army of regular people (page 18)

pamphlet — (PAM-flit) a short paper that often discusses current events or ideas (page 13)

Patriot — (PAY-tree-uht) a colonist who wanted freedom from British rule (page 10)

protest — (proh-TEHST) (verb) to say that you do not think that something is right; to disagree (page 8)

protest — (PROH-tehst) (noun) a public demonstration showing that people do not agree with something (page 8)

rebel — (rih-BEHL) (verb) to fight against the laws of a person in power (page 3)

rebel — (REH-buhl) (noun) someone who does not obey a person in power (page 6)

INDEX

Solve This

Answers
1. Page 8
   90,000 pounds
2. Page 25
   $80.04